Let Freedom Ring

William Penn

Founder of the Pennsylvania Colony

by Bernadette L. Baczynski

Consultant:
Wayne Bodle
Assistant Professor of History
Indiana University of Pennsylvania
Indiana, Pennsylvania

Capstone press
Mankato, Minnesota

Capstone Press
151 Good Counsel Drive • P.O. Box 669 • Mankato, Minnesota 56002
www.capstonepub.com

Books published by Capstone Press are manufactured with paper
containing at least 10 percent post-consumer waste.

Library of Congress Cataloging-in-Publication Data
Baczynski, Bernadette L.
    William Penn: founder of the Pennsylvania Colony / by Bernadette Baczynski.
    p. cm.——(Let freedom ring)
    Summary: A biography of the religious leader and founder of the Pennsylvania Colony,
whose Quaker beliefs helped him form peaceful relationships with the American Indians
and lay the foundation of religious freedom in America.
    Includes bibliographical references and index.
    ISBN-13: 978-0-7368-2459-0 (Hardcover)   ISBN-10: 0-7368-2459-6 (Hardcover)
    ISBN-13: 978-0-7368-4486-4 (Paperback)   ISBN-10: 0-7368-4486-4 (Paperback)
    1. Penn, William, 1644–1718—Juvenile literature. 2. Pioneers—Pennsylvania—
Biography—Juvenile literature. 3. Quakers—Pennsylvania—Biography—Juvenile literature.
4. Pennsylvania—History—Colonial period, ca. 1600–1775—Juvenile literature. [1. Penn,
William, 1644–1718. 2. Pioneers. 3. Quakers. 4. Pennsylvania—History—Colonial period,
ca. 1600–1775.] I. Title. II. Series.
F152.2.B13 2004
974.8'02'092—dc22   2003013122

Editorial Credits
Donald Lemke, editor; Kia Adams, series designer; Enoch Peterson, book designer;
    Jo Miller and Wanda Winch, photo researchers; Eric Kudalis, product planning editor

Photo Credits
Art Resource/The New York Public Library, 21, 32
Brian Hunt & Pennsylvania Capitol Preservation Committee, 7
Bridgeman Art Library/John Noott Galleries, Broadway, Worcestershire, UK, 17
Corbis/Francis G. Mayer, 29; Patrick Ward, 41
Courtesy of The Historical Society of Pennsylvania Collection, Atwater Kent Museum
    of Philadelphia, 26
Friends Historical Library of Swarthmore College, 13
Getty Images Inc./Hulton/Archive, cover, 9, 14, 34, 39
North Wind Picture Archives, 11, 18, 22, 27, 42 (top and bottom)
Pennsylvania Historical & Museum Commission, 36
Photri-Microstock, 25
Richard Cummins, 5
Stock Montage Inc., 31

Printed in the United States of America in Stevens Point, Wisconsin.
022011   006090R

Table of Contents

Features

Chapter One

A Powerful Message

When William Penn was 12 years old, his family moved into a three-story castle in Ireland. The castle towered over an old village of thatched-roof cottages. Huge forests and hills surrounded the small community. **Peasants** and villagers farmed these fertile lands.

Penn enjoyed living a quiet life in the country. His private tutor kept him busy with studies. When he was not studying, his father taught him how to hunt and help manage the property.

One day, a traveling preacher came to the small village. His name was Thomas Loe. He was part of a new religious group called the **Quakers**. Loe was known for his booming voice and inspirational speeches. People gathered in large numbers to hear his powerful message.

Macroom Castle was William Penn's childhood home. Part of it still stands in the western part of Macroom, Ireland.

In His Own Words

"The country life is to be preferred, for there we see the works of God, but in cities little else but the works of men. And one makes a better subject for our contemplation than the other."

—William Penn, *Some Fruits of Solitude*, 1693

Penn's father was curious and invited the preacher to speak at the castle. When the day came, many people crowded into a large room in the castle. Villagers, staff members, army troops, and the entire Penn family waited. Soon, Loe began to tell about the loving presence of God in every person. He called this presence the Inner Light. Loe believed that the Inner Light would help people live with peace, honesty, and kindness toward others. These qualities were what mattered in God's eyes, said Loe. People who lived by the Inner Light had no place for war or fighting.

Penn and the others listened as Loe continued his message of brotherhood and peace. Many people in the crowd became emotional and started to cry. William was only 12 years old. Although he may not have realized at the time, his life had been changed forever.

Throughout his life, Penn wrote about his thoughts and experiences.

Chapter Two

Early Life and Education

On October 14, 1644, William Penn was born in London, England. He was the first of Sir William and Margaret Penn's three children. The Penn family was respected and fairly wealthy. Penn's father was a property owner and an admiral in the Royal Navy of England.

Penn was a curious boy and a good student. When he was 11 years old, Penn attended Chigwell Academy near Wanstead, England. In 1656, his family moved to Ireland, where he was privately tutored.

In 1660, Penn entered Oxford University. Shortly after arriving at the school, Penn became troubled. He disagreed with the rule that every student must belong to the Church of England. He believed that students should have the right to choose their own religion.

Penn's father, Sir William Penn, was a wealthy and respected admiral in the Royal Navy of England.

In 1662, Penn left Oxford University. He told his father that he had been thrown out of the school.

Penn's father was upset. He sent Penn to France to learn about manners and foreign affairs. While in France, Penn studied for 18 months at a religious school. In 1664, Penn returned to London. He was well educated and dressed in fine French clothing.

Even after returning from France, Penn still had a desire to learn. In 1665, he entered law school. Before the end of his first semester, England went to war against Holland. Penn decided to join his father in the navy.

After a few weeks aboard a navy ship, Penn returned to England. He went back to school. In the spring of 1665, the school closed because of a deadly disease called the plague.

In the fall, Penn's father needed someone to manage the family's home in Ireland. He asked Penn to help. Penn agreed to leave school for good and take care of the property.

Becoming a Quaker

In 1667, Penn heard Thomas Loe speak again. Penn was now 23 years old. The Quaker preacher inspired him. This time, Loe's simple lifestyle and message of equality grabbed Penn's attention. Penn soon became a Quaker.

Penn briefly served in the navy before becoming a Quaker. While in the navy at age 22, he posed for this portrait in his suit of armor.

The Quakers

Members of the Religious Society of Friends were also called Quakers. They believed in the Bible. They also believed that everyone has an Inner Light, or a basic goodness. This Inner Light inspires people to serve God. Unlike other church services, Quaker meetings were simple gatherings. They did not have rituals or a set program. Quakers believed in the equality of all people. They were also **pacifists** who did not believe in war.

During this time, many Quakers were punished for their beliefs. They were often arrested, **banished**, or even killed. Penn was sent to prison many times for his beliefs. He did not use his wealth or power to get special treatment. During one nine-month stay in prison, Penn began to write *No Cross, No Crown*. This book established rules for Quaker behavior and simple living.

On September 16, 1670, Penn's father died. Admiral William Penn left his son a large amount of money and property. He also left an uncollected debt from King Charles II of England. The king owed Penn's father 16,000 pounds.

A Time for Change

On April 4, 1672, Penn married Gulielma Springett. Soon, the couple tried to have children. Unfortunately, their first three babies died.

Even during hard times, Penn's wife, Gulielma Springett, supported his Quaker beliefs.

Father of the Quakers

George Fox (1624–1691) was born into a poor family in Fenny Drayton, a town in Leicestershire, England. As a boy, he learned how to become a shoemaker. The young man became interested in religion.

Fox grew tired of the bad habits and scandals in his family's church. He believed people should show their faith through good deeds. In 1647, Fox helped found the Religious Society of Friends, also known as Quakers. For the rest of his life, Fox spread the Quaker message of peace.

On January 25, 1676, Penn and Gulielma finally had a healthy child. They named him Springett.

In the late 1600s, Penn started to encourage Quakerism in other parts of Europe. His trips around the area cost money, and the Penns' fortunes began to suffer. Penn had to sell some of his properties to support the family.

Around the same time, Penn helped settle a land dispute between two Quakers. The men wanted to start a settlement in the western part of New Jersey. Penn helped write the Concessions and Agreements. This document laid out a plan for the colony's government. It covered many groundbreaking issues, such as freedom of speech and freedom of religion. The document would later become a model for Pennsylvania's government.

Chapter Three

The Pennsylvania Colony

Penn wanted to establish a colony for Quakers. In 1680, he finally asked King Charles II to pay back his father's debt. Surprisingly, the king granted his request. On March 4, 1681, King Charles II signed the Charter of Pennsylvania. This document gave Penn an area of land west of the Delaware River in North America.

In exchange for the land, the king asked for one-fifth of all the gold and silver from the new colony. He also asked for two beaver skins to be delivered every year to his castle. It was a small price.

A New Colony

It would be one and a half years before Penn would visit his new colony. In the meantime, he started planning for his arrival. He wrote a letter to the people already settled in the area of the Pennsylvania Colony.

In this painting by Allan Stewart (1865–1951), William Penn, right, receives the Charter of Pennsylvania from King Charles II of England.

Did You Know?

Penn wanted to name his new colony New Wales or Sylvania. He was afraid to put "Penn" in the name. Penn did not want people to think that he had named the colony for himself. King Charles II, shown at right, wanted to honor Penn's late father. He insisted on naming the colony Pennsylvania, meaning Penn's woods.

In his letter to the settlers, Penn explained his ideas for the new colony. He wanted the settlers to live free and make their own laws. These ideas became part of Penn's plan for the government of Pennsylvania.

Penn wanted the Pennsylvania Colony to have a government where one person did not run the whole colony. He wrote the Frame of Government, which included 40 laws. This document promised fair treatment for everyone. It guaranteed rights for women, public education for children, and freedom of worship.

The City of Brotherly Love

Penn also made plans for the capital of Pennsylvania. He named the city Philadelphia, which means "city of brotherly love."

Penn wanted to build Philadelphia between the Delaware and Schuylkill Rivers. The area had a long waterfront where ships could land. He also planned a center square for a state house and other public buildings. Two wide avenues would divide Philadelphia into four equal sections.

The Philadelphia Plan

Penn based his plan for the city of Philadelphia on ideas used in London. These ideas had been developed after the Great Fire in 1666, which destroyed most of London. The city's cramped and crowded layout helped the fire spread quickly. Afterward, several architects recommended that London be rebuilt with a more modern and open pattern. This pattern included wide streets and green spaces. In 1681, Penn used the idea to design Philadelphia. Since then, many American cities have copied this plan.

Penn left room for parks and houses with big yards. He even named the streets himself. Philadelphia was Penn's ideal city.

Coming to America

In 1682, Penn left Gulielma and his children in England and sailed for North America. The trip aboard the ship *Welcome* took more than two months.

On October 27, 1682, Penn finally arrived in the area of Pennsylvania. The land was even better than he had imagined. It had huge forests and a large supply of food and game.

While sailing to North America, William Penn, shown at right, and other leaders discussed plans for the Pennsylvania Colony.

On October 27, 1682, Penn, with arm raised, landed in the area of Pennsylvania. The young Quaker quickly established a government in the new colony.

In His Own Words

"There can be no friendship where there is no freedom. Friendship loves a free air, and will not be penned up in straight and narrow enclosures."

—William Penn, *Some Fruits of Solitude*, 1693

Penn immediately went to work. He visited with the governors of neighboring colonies and called together the first assembly. Eventually, the assembly approved his Frame of Government.

Settlers continued to arrive in the new colony. They trusted Penn's promise of freedom of worship. Penn tried to make room for the new settlers. He bought land from the American Indians in the area. The new land increased the size of the colony.

Chapter Four

Penn and the American Indians

Unlike many settlers, Penn believed in treating the American Indians fairly. Before he arrived in Pennsylvania, Penn sent a letter to the American Indians in the area. He wrote, "I desire to enjoy [the land] with your love and consent, that we may always live together as neighbors and friends."

The Great Treaty of Shackamaxon

Penn tried to pay the American Indians a fair price for the land. He wanted them to know that the Quakers were peaceful and honorable. The Great Treaty of Shackamaxon in 1682 helped create peaceful dealings with the Lenni Lenape, also known as the Delaware Indians.

William Penn, shown here with the Charter of Pennsylvania, lived peacefully with the American Indians in the area.

Wampum Belt

Some American Indians made **wampum** belts as a reminder of events such as treaties. Today, visitors to the Atwater Kent Museum of Philadelphia can see an original wampum belt, pictured below. This belt was given to Penn at Shackamaxon in 1682.

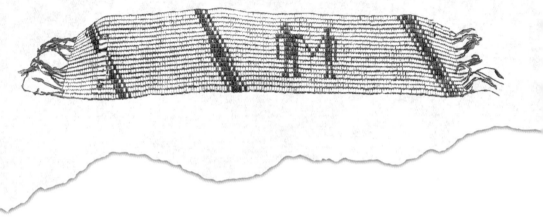

The Great Treaty resulted from a meeting between Penn, other settlers, and the Lenni Lenape. The meeting took place near Philadelphia in Shackamaxon. During the meeting, Penn promised that Quakers and American Indians would always be friends. The Great Treaty of Shackamaxon is the only treaty between American Indians and settlers that was never broken.

In 1682, Penn and other settlers met with Lenni Lenape Indians to sign the Great Treaty of Shackamaxon.

Brother *Onas*

American Indians gave William Penn a special nickname. They observed that white men used a goose **quill** as a pen. Although their language did not have a word for pen, *onas* meant quill. Soon, the American Indians called Penn "Brother *Onas.*"

Respecting the American Indians

Quakers usually made decisions as a group. American Indians approached their problems in a similar manner. The chief sat in the middle of the group. Then, he would ask for advice from both old and young people. Decisions could take weeks or even months. Penn respected the American Indian process and never hurried the decisions.

Penn admired the way American Indians lived as a community. He got along with the American Indians and treated them fairly. Penn walked among them without weapons or guards. He was not afraid.

Penn also participated in their games and customs. He learned their language and brought them gifts. Because he respected the American Indian cultures, Penn's two-year stay in the Pennsylvania Colony was peaceful.

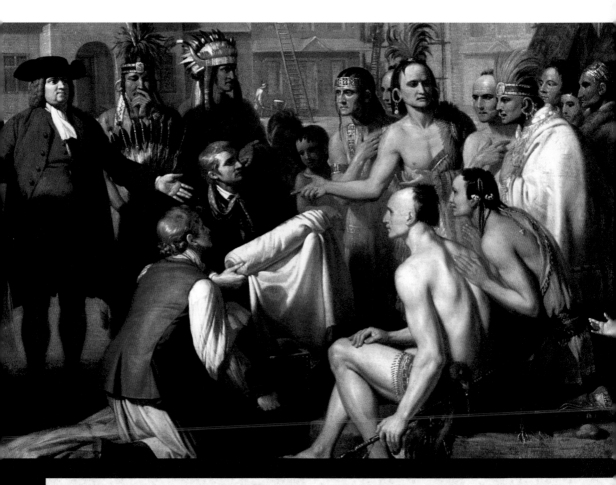

Penn, far left, and other Quakers respected American Indians in the area of Pennsylvania. They often brought gifts and made peaceful decisions.

Chapter Five

The Long Voyage Home

Penn had one problem he could not solve alone. The area between the colonies of Pennsylvania and Maryland had never been accurately surveyed. Charles Calvert, the third Lord Baltimore of Maryland, questioned the boundary line between the two colonies. No one knew for sure who owned the land or who had the right to sell it.

Penn and Lord Baltimore decided to write to the king. They hoped he would settle the matter. After a year without an answer, both men decided to speak with the king personally.

On August 12, 1684, Penn set sail from Philadelphia to London. He expected to return to North America with his family.

Penn made several long voyages across the Atlantic Ocean. In 1684, he sailed back to London to settle a land dispute and be with his family.

By 1685, the border dispute was temporarily solved. Penn and Lord Baltimore split the land in half. Unfortunately, it would be 15 years before Penn would return to the Pennsylvania Colony.

A Man of Sorrows

Unlike most men in England, Penn had access to the king. His relationship with King Charles II had been good. But things were different when Penn returned to England. The government had many problems. Many Quakers were in prison for their beliefs.

Penn, seated, and Lord Baltimore argued over the boundary between the colonies of Pennsylvania and Maryland.

On February 6, 1685, King Charles II died. His brother, James II, was crowned king. James had been Penn's boyhood friend. The new king wanted to work toward religious freedom in England. In 1687, James set free thousands of religious prisoners, including many Quakers.

In 1688, James was overthrown during the Glorious Revolution (1688–1689). James quickly fled to France. William III, ruler of the Netherlands, and his wife Mary II took control of England. The new rulers did not agree with James' decisions or beliefs.

The new rulers suspected that Penn was still loyal to James. In 1689, Penn was arrested for **treason**, or trying to overthrow the government. He was imprisoned in the Tower of London for two weeks. King William also took possession of the Pennsylvania Colony.

After being released, Penn went into hiding and worked to clear his name. He had time to reflect on his beliefs during these troubled years. He wrote several thoughtful works, including *Some Fruits of Solitude.*

After three long years, Penn's name was cleared. Unfortunately, his wife Gulielma had become ill. On February 23, 1694, she died in Penn's arms.

A New Beginning

Soon, Penn's luck changed for the better. In 1694, King William gave Pennsylvania back to him. Penn also met Hannah Callowhill. She was the daughter of old Quaker friends. On March 5, 1696, they were married. Eventually, the couple had seven children.

On March 5, 1696, Penn married Hannah Callowhill in a Quaker wedding.

It would be three more years before the family would sail to Pennsylvania. In the meantime, Penn asked a fellow Quaker to handle his money in England. Philip Ford made Penn sign promises to repay him for salary and services.

In Pennsylvania, there were problems between Quakers and non-Quakers. The return to the colony could wait no longer. In September 1699, Penn and his family sailed for North America.

Back in Philadelphia

Philadelphia was a much different place when Penn arrived. It was now the second-largest city in the colonies. Only Boston, Massachusetts, was larger. Philadelphia had more than 5,000 people and 700 brick houses.

The growing colony also had many problems. There was tension between Quakers and the other settlers. Pirates who sailed along the coast often seized English ships bringing goods to the colonies. Penn believed the colonies could work together and solve these problems. The governors of the other colonies agreed. Penn sent his plan to the king.

The king was more worried about the threat of war in Europe. He was sure the wars would spread to the colonies. Since the Quakers did not believe in fighting, he knew Pennsylvania would not supply soldiers or weapons for a war. The king began to think about taking control of Pennsylvania.

In November 1701, the Penn family left their country home at Pennsbury Manor. They began their voyage back across the Atlantic Ocean. Once again, Penn returned to London to talk with the king. He convinced the king to let him keep Pennsylvania.

A re-creation of Pennsbury Manor allows visitors at Morrisville, Pennsylvania, to experience Penn's country home.

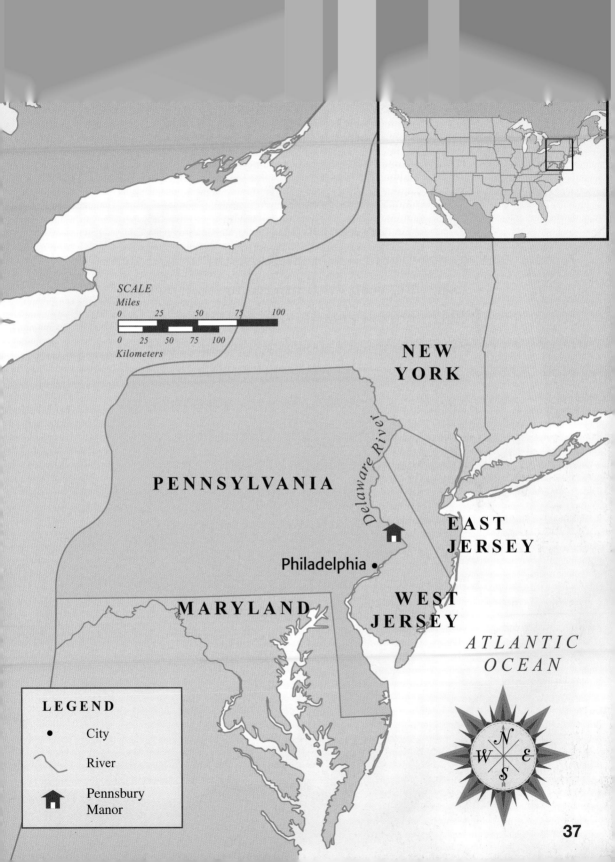

SCALE

Miles

0   25   50   75   100

0   25   50   75   100

Kilometers

NEW YORK

PENNSYLVANIA

Delaware River

EAST JERSEY

Philadelphia •

WEST JERSEY

MARYLAND

ATLANTIC OCEAN

LEGEND

•   City

⌇   River

🏠   Pennsbury Manor

Chapter Six

Later Years

Penn never returned to the colony of Pennsylvania. Through the years, he had signed many contracts with his business manager Philip Ford. Penn did not carefully examine these documents. It was a mistake. Ford was a greedy man. He wanted as much of Penn's fortune as he could get. After Ford died, his family sued Penn. They wanted Penn to pay them the money he owed Ford.

Penn could not pay the large amount of money. In 1708, he was sent to prison for almost a year in the Tower of London. Penn's many friends came to his aid. The matters were eventually settled, but Penn was never the same. He was growing tired and ill.

During the later years of his life, Penn started having health problems
and was no longer full of energy.

Modern Quakers

Today, almost 300,000 Quakers live throughout the world. Some of these Quakers have had a big impact on the history of the United States. Famous Quakers include Presidents Richard Nixon and Herbert Hoover, first lady Dolley Madison, and suffragist Susan B. Anthony. Members of the Religious Society of Friends continue to work to eliminate poverty and achieve peace.

In 1712, Penn suffered several **strokes**. For the rest of his life, he needed to be cared for by others. His memory, speech, and strength faded. On July 30, 1718, Penn died at home. He was 73 years old.

William Penn's Legacy

Penn's generous nature and his visionary spirit helped build the United States. Pennsylvania Colony was the first example of people governing themselves in North America. Parts of the Frame of Government became a model for the state constitutions of Pennsylvania and the Constitution of the United States. By the time of the Revolutionary War (1775–1783), Philadelphia had become America's largest city. During these early years, it also served as the capital of the United States. Today, the city continues to be a center for art and industry. People can walk the streets where America was born and trace Penn's path to freedom.

Today, a 37-foot (11-meter) statue of William Penn overlooks downtown Philadelphia. It is the tallest statue on any building in the world.

TIME LINE

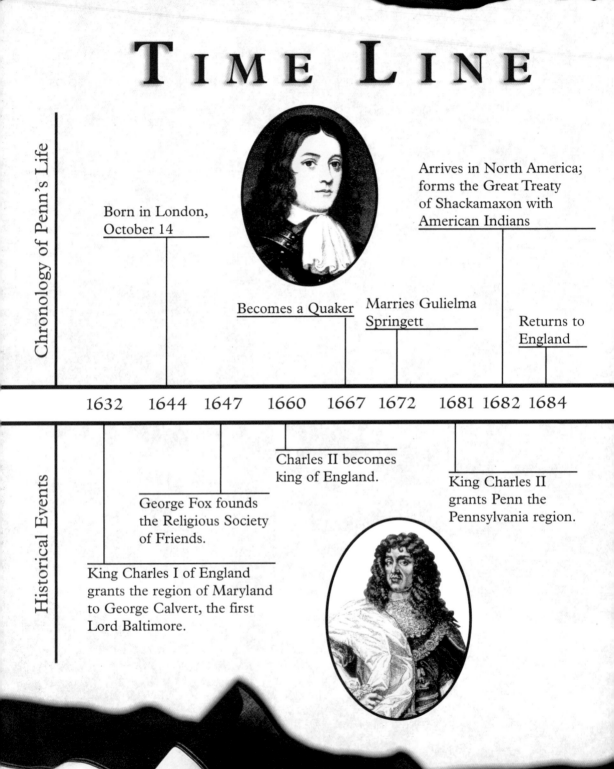

Chronology of Penn's Life

Born in London, October 14

Arrives in North America; forms the Great Treaty of Shackamaxon with American Indians

Becomes a Quaker

Marries Gulielma Springett

Returns to England

1632　1644　1647　1660　1667　1672　1681　1682　1684

Historical Events

Charles II becomes king of England.

George Fox founds the Religious Society of Friends.

King Charles II grants Penn the Pennsylvania region.

King Charles I of England grants the region of Maryland to George Calvert, the first Lord Baltimore.

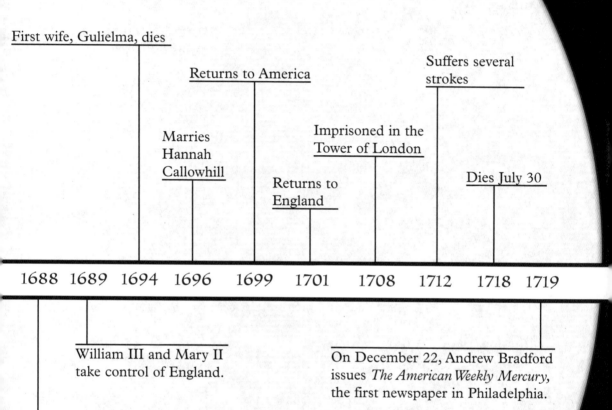

First wife, Gulielma, dies

Returns to America

Suffers several strokes

Marries
Hannah
Callowhill

Imprisoned in the
Tower of London

Returns to
England

Dies July 30

| 1688 | 1689 | 1694 | 1696 | 1699 | 1701 | 1708 | 1712 | 1718 | 1719 |

William III and Mary II
take control of England.

On December 22, Andrew Bradford
issues *The American Weekly Mercury,*
the first newspaper in Philadelphia.

The Glorious Revolution
begins; King James II is
overthrown and escapes
to France.

Glossary

banish (BAN-ish)—to send someone away from a place and order the person not to return

pacifist (PASS-uh-fist)—someone who strongly believes that war and violence are wrong and refuses to fight

peasant (PEZ-uhnt)—someone who owns a small farm or works on a farm, especially in Europe and some Asian countries

Quaker (KWAY-kur)—a member of the Religious Society of Friends, a religious group founded in the 1600s that prefers simple religious services and opposes war

quill (KWIL)—the long hollow part in the center of a bird's feather; a quill can be carved to make a pen.

stroke (STROHK)—a medical condition caused by a sudden lack of oxygen to the brain; a stroke can cause loss of memory, speech, and strength.

treason (TREE-zuhn)—betraying one's country, especially by helping the enemy or plotting to overthrow the government

wampum (WAHM-puhm)—beads made from polished shells strung together or woven to make belts

Read More

Glaser, Jason. *Pennsylvania.* Land of Liberty. Mankato, Minn.: Capstone Press, 2004.

Kroll, Steven. *William Penn, Founder of Pennsylvania.* New York: Holiday House, 2000.

Lutz, Norma Jean. *William Penn: Founder of Democracy.* Colonial Leaders. Philadelphia: Chelsea House, 2000.

Somervill, Barbara A. *Pennsylvania.* From Sea to Shining Sea. New York: Children's Press, 2002.

Swain, Gwenyth. *Freedom Seeker: A Story About William Penn.* A Creative Minds Biography. Minneapolis: Carolrhoda Books, 2003.

Useful Addresses

The Atwater Kent Museum of Philadelphia

15 South Seventh Street
Philadelphia, PA 19106
Founded over 60 years ago, the Atwater Kent Museum allows children and adults to experience the history of Philadelphia.

Independence National Historical Park

143 South Third Street
Philadelphia, PA 19106
Located in downtown Philadelphia, the park gives visitors a chance to experience the history of Philadelphia and is home to the Liberty Bell and Independence Hall.

Pennsbury Manor

400 Pennsbury Manor Road
Morrisville, PA 19067
Located in Buck's County, Pennsylvania, William Penn's country home has been re-created to provide visitors with a sense of life in the 1600s.

Internet Sites

FactHound offers a safe, fun way to find Internet sites related to this book. All of the sites on FactHound have been researched by our staff.

Here's how:
1. Visit *www.facthound.com*
2. Type in this special code **0736824596** for age-appropriate sites. Or enter a search word related to this book for a more general search.
3. Click on the **Fetch It** button.

FactHound will fetch the best sites for you!

Index